LOOKING INTO THE DEEP END

David Sweetman

LOOKING INTO
THE DEEP END

FABER AND FABER
London   Boston

First published in 1981
by Faber and Faber Limited
3 Queen Square London WC1N 3AU
Printed in Great Britain by
Latimer Trend & Company Ltd Plymouth
All rights reserved

British Library Cataloguing in Publication Data

Sweetman, David
  Looking into the deep end.
  I. Title
  821'.9'14   PR6069.W3/

  ISBN 0-571-11730-9

for Vatcharin Bhumichitr

Contents

Acknowledgements are due to the following where many of these poems appeared for the first time: *Bananas*, *Encounter*, *Hibernia*, the *Listener*, the *New Statesman*, *Quarto* and *The Times Literary Supplement*.

THE ART OF POTTERY   1945

Teabowl and vase, tray and ewer
stacked in the studio like shapes
fragmented from a landscape: sky
cloudy over the three-colour glazes,
a beach on the crackled oatmeal,
slow seas passing through and across
the rough biscuit—all moods of the tide.

For forty years, Kenji has drawn
melting hands from the grey slip,
begun creation with the actions of death,
seeming to strangle the reluctant clay
until it yields, suddenly,
as if responding to his impatient foot
stamping, stamping, the clacking treddle.

Today is the never-tired-of moment,
the bank-vault kiln reopened.
And yet, this once, heat and shine
are nothing when behind him breaks a light
brighter than the city's million filaments,
uncountable neon-signs squandering rainbows,
that stripes Kenji the cold white

and midnight blue of a mackerel's belly.
And as this light leaves him,
sagging like a tired dish,
his shadow settles on the nearest bowl
with the merest stroke, almost a letter,
the beginnings of a haiku perhaps
or the fringe of a wave by Hiroshige . . .

THE LONG DAYS

They gave you a world smelling of leather,
continents like twisted stairs
and told you to kick it
away down the lane that marks
the suburbs' end, an explorer's vague line,
the convenient lie beyond which
a terra incognita beckons.

There, amongst the farmyard's aimlessness,
a disconnected pig lazes
its two-pin snout unplugged,
while a cow crooks its tail
like a duchess' finger
then craps like an old drunk.
Back at the house nature is more serious:

the young bitch shaking out
three clenched fists secretly under a bed
or the silent, Egyptian pose
of the old lady on the chesterfield.
Where have you been? she asks softly.
You shake your head, afraid to inhale
the embalming sweetness of camphor.

Her hand tries to mould her head
on those days when she sings to herself
and sometimes when the tears come
they roll from her eyes
like steel balls in a penny arcade.
They too reflect lies, bending
the cupboards, warping the chairs.

SAY IT WITH FLOWERS

Correctly placed, five tulips will
swell and narrow from stem to flower
echoing their own unopened heads.

So far tight-lipped and secretive
they suddenly spread into green flame
and Ottoman courtiers dance upon the pyre.

It cannot last, a green back bends in prayer,
red trumpets try to sound the sultan to his mosque
but they're a dying breed whose empire falls silent—

the green tongues hang, the petals curl
into a caricature of hate finally liver-lipped
like Streicher, a mirror to his own imagined Jew.

And yet we bear them home like torches.

COASTING

There is a climate of failure,
clouds imploded like useless chimney stacks,
while on the beach the sandworms
put out spaghetti for the neighbours
though no one eats.
A lazy length of hawser can't spell
even one of the names of Allah correctly
and there's the sinking feeling that comes
from seeing the lifeboat tracks going on and on
into the water, tramlines to Atlantis.

Like the bored teenagers on the promenade
the sea too keeps trying to run away,
off to London and the bright lights,
but always failing, failing, failing . . .
Always pulling back at the last moment.

THE UNHAPPY INVENTOR*

I remember Uncle August, such a poet,
trying to create the indestructible being
he'd collage the objects from his pockets,
seeing the zippo lighter as an angry mouth

to be calmed with a whistle then laid beneath
his folded pebble spectacles *et voilà*
a face, gawping but silent. Unlike my aunt
who noisily upbraided him for his fantasies—

the device that gave our parakeet
a cautious freedom on a string whose ratchet
could reel her safely home, until she wove a dream
of flight that bound us all in its web and worse,

shattered a vase. But *he* was made for kids,
pasting photographs from magazines for us.
Once he made the skinless man, gleaming
French horn intestines, crash-helmet skull,

xylophone ribs and angle-poise limbs,
for everything was something else
in Uncle August's world of metal metaphors.
And yet, unhappy inventor that he was,

he sensed that love and forgiveness
are not to be made of washers and wire
and these he found only with us, the adults
despised him, my father thought him mad.

*Based on the painting *Remember Uncle August the unhappy inventor* by George Grosz

13

He died one Christmas with us all at the house
and I crept into his room to see the final creation
where his left hand had moulded a ridged square
on the counterpane that looked like a stockade

in which a lone cowboy could make a last stand.
Later in life I discovered how famous he'd been,
how, during the War, he'd invented a bomb
that ricocheted across entire cities, leaving

only charred creatures and split stones
in its fiery wake, and yet his inspiration
had been his daughters playing ball
in the yard. After Dresden

he made nothing more than amusements for us
and listened silently to his wife's complaints
while turning his wedding ring round and round
as if to somehow lower the volume.

CITY GARDEN EPITOME

This piazza's a room with a hundred windows
opening inwards and, on a bench, an old lady
plaiting spaghetti with a chopstick in each hand.

Then a girl comes looking for someone who's gone
and when her eyes perspire, the old men shiver
huddling up to the bulrush's one-bar fire.

CREATIVE ACTS

... tell me how you seek and I will tell you what you seek ...

WITTGENSTEIN

I INSIGHT

A blind man sits for his portrait:
eyes the colour of troubled waters,
he finds no shore and his hand
comforts only an imaginary child.

Watching him carefully, the painter
fences with insanely coloured guano
until, tired of vision, he gently sets
his wooden heart upon a table.

Winter elms are the nervous system
of the sky but the artist sees only
the window's mollusc trails. Yet,
behind drawn curtains, the sitter

can see fire glowing in his veins,
can lovingly rub his eyes
till galaxies of colours come
in search of which all artists fail.

Another day, he'll touch his image,
feel blizzards of paint, hard
as braille typed by jailed murderers
bringing Milton to sightless souls.

2 CONCRETE POEM

The architect failed to see the curl of iron hair
that embraced his papers or the way a mapping-nib
resembled a bishop's mitre, plotting instead

a Home for the Aged like stacked coffins,
a white cross at every window's angle,
a staircase that draws a question-mark

as if the roof has doubts. So when the day dies,
and his glass tower inherits the clouds,
they wrap the clerks in woolly dreams of work's end

while the last one alive, the post boy, drinks
from a water-fountain, an aquarium of ghost fish,
and stares out at a neighbouring tower reflecting

his own which must mirror the other as if all distance
were a fading heresy that he could rise above
in that spirited apotheosis of the bubbles in the bowl.

3 PUTTING UP THE SHUTTERS

The Hindenburg's discarded cigar butt
scattering a colony of ants
and the five frantic elves
setting up the Iwo Jima golf-course,
that Vietcong face, distorted as if a great wind
rushes from the revolver at his temple
and the weeping wraith, haunting
the petrified forest of the Orly crash, deceive:

the cloud over Hiroshima
and the magnified corona when a drop of liquid
strikes the taut convexity of still water

are equally beautiful. *A mushroom*, we say,
though a moment earlier, the deadly dust
consumed itself like old men's lips.
Perhaps those alien tribes were right,
these cameras only take, and take . . .

4 STORIES TO FRIGHTEN CHILDREN WITH

Remember the Spartan boy, a snapping fox in his lap
curled as if his own guts had spilled out, grown hairy?
Today it shines in metal coils, sprouts wires, is hugged

by a lad in black nourishing a foetal terror silently.
But others speak, myths are made—in an Asian city,
tarts wound themselves with lipstick, impatient

for the crew shooting a recent war. Away on location,
a make-up girl squints at a photograph
before painting the acne of napalm on a child's face.

5 ECOLE DE SOHO

In the rank stairwell, the other kids
aerosolled vast cocks like ships' cannon
and tits with eyes that followed you round,
while Ben drew his dreams on envelopes
and ran away to make them true.

No one bothered to report the matter
and he found cinemas, highly individual,
where amateurs of the art come to recall
the avant-garde, that frameless picture
in the dark whose cubist bodies interlock.

Artists of the pissoir, they beg a ride
waving a soft hitch-hiker's thumb.
Like Ben's worst patron who laid him
on a rented bed, seeing the first Picasso,
blue in twenty watt chiaroscuro.

* * *

The psychiatrists said: *Draw anything*.
But when he drew a pop-star, mouthing
into a handmike, they saw obsessions,
oral and male, and tried electric shocks.
Now Ben paints walls as white as his mind.

INSIDE OUT

She operates carelessly on an omelette,
attention wandering from television
to window where three hovering sparrows
mock the ducks on the flowering wall.

For everything is inside out today:
the gin bottle is frozen water carved
at attention yet white fluff settles
warmly on the street lamp's shoulder.

Inside, a riot happens, shots are fired.
One tie-dyes a grocer's window,
another pins a rose on a man's shirt
which he cups to him like a gentle secret.

She turns away, aware of her spectacles
as if the world had shrunk its horizons,
while before her the yellow ectoplasm
forms the outline of a face she had loved.

Suddenly, war breaks out, shells exploding
like surfacing whales, but she eats greedily
until all that's left is a wet plate
or the aerial photo of an Asian delta.

THE NORTH THAT EVERY PILLOW KNOWS

Without outward declarations, who can conclude an inward love?
JOHN DONNE

Out of darkness, miners stare like Coptic saints
while pyramids of slag recall an older idolatry
that enslaved their fathers. Boot caps rise

as if the wet cobbles dance before them, they seldom speak,
the barman knows their beer, they never touch,
the hands around each glass are the separate hemispheres

of a globe that can't be one. This is the North to me,
strong men and unacknowledged love,
where every man hears the other home, tap-tapping

like a hammer at the face, though breath comes
louder than the shunting wagons, and where each sees
the helmet lamps wink down the rows, stars

freed from dead rock, doomed to fade
when the pit-wheel hauls up a sun to wake the wives
who'll hang out sheets as bunting for its light.

BURNING A BABY

The ribs on the fallen leaves were gathered as wings
protective of a little torso, yet we broke them underfoot
until the crematorium threatened its abusive furniture:

the lectern's whipping post, lamps swung on chains,
hassocks bound with thongs for you, the victim
whimpering through your lacy gag, staring

at the wooden boat we had brought, so frail that when
the vicar poked a finger it sank with a slow leak.
Freed, we saw smoke corkscrewing the sky, opening rain,

the window of the hirecar wept for us and every tree
into the city aborted leaves to soften our journey.
You kept one, lobes like the three stumpy fingers

on all the cartoon creatures that kids love. That leaf too,
lived short of nine months and showed the same
russet, autumnal stains as the surgeon's green gown.

POINTS AND SIGNALS

I am a city dweller now
and see things differently, wondering
why these young farmers are so improvident
building houses of glass and straw, ignoring
the solid stone their fathers left.

Every train ride is the trial of the nineteenth century,
guilty of ugliness, guilty of waste,
yet the abandoned lots pretend to a gentler age
with artificial ponds and ruined follies.
Later, the landscape flattens, the journey tires

until, like flak in old war movies, sodium lamps
fall away into the coming night. Heavy as Gibbon
this darkness too has sudden insights—
the man in the parallel universe, remembering
the boy who took the Scotsman to London,

saw four museums in a day and hung from the gods
as if the opera were a well;
though that was before my body became a face
with sad-eyed nipples, navel huffing and blowing
like a tired putto. Without warning,

a station! And there in the brightness
another boy looks in where I had been.
He stares at me and I know all his dreams
and long to open a window to tell him
that the city waits. But this is a sealed train

bearing the bacillus of the future
safely away from these Northern folk;
leaving them to wonder. Mindlessly my hands touch
the glass but, mistaking the gesture, the boy
waves goodbye and follows as the train moves on.

SAIDI'S WIFE

Often Africa seemed quite empty,
the shadows of walls lay on dust roads
sharp and vacant like Nubian pyramids.

Stepping through them, Saidi's wife
would slowly cross our compound
fruit punctuating her scrubbed tray,
adjusting and readjusting the *kanga*
that half-veiled her face, blushing feet
slapping the earth. Then suddenly
a glimpse of nipple,
black as a missionary's biretta.

One day there was gunfire,
no more than the spit and cackle of ice
dashed with strong spirits,
though less than a mile away people died.
As usual Saidi's family worked their fields
so that at any hour the village seemed forgotten,
the thatched huts lying as still as shells
clustered in an abandoned rockpool.

When night came, the palm tree's rotor-blades
whipped up a wind, bamboo telescopes searched
out the stars, and always an electric voice sang
loud but unseen, somewhere in the listening bush.

LOOKING INTO THE DEEP END

A boy from a village
a nation away from deep water, to him
this was a fascinating parcel, crumpled paper
surface, reflections of ravelled string

though strangely empty. Called
by god knows what palaeozoic urge
he'd stripped and lowered himself in
then tried to walk a length.

But here was no gentle slope, this drop
sharp to the diver's end.
I ran up as they pulled him out, stopping
not at the baby-drool from mouth and nose

more at the darkness, a shadow
between his legs suggesting the outline of Africa,
that brought back those guilty explorations
of childhood that boys share, raising too

a day when I watched my father turn a stone
as if slowly opening a child's sarcophagus, empty
except for the blue-grey woodlice
lying like ampoules pallid with imagined sins—

all hastily reinterred again,
for when they had tidied away
the drowned boy, I dived cleanly
into the deep end and the world,

to my lensless eyes, returned
to that innocent game of green-tiled chess
that sun and water play
with boneless, shifting pieces.

COLONIAL MARRIAGE

The crickets type with one finger
a message that infuriates the ghekkos
who wriggle from their underwear and dive
into the shipless seas behind the prints.

On her dressing-table the city of the future
smells good yet insects strafe its empty streets.

Her clenched fist raised against the moon
is a glove puppet speaking in the near dawn
of escape! But the bed is a parcel wrapped
in mosquito net, sent far from happiness.

He is so thin and white, hair trailing away,
she thinks of boiled leek or a favourite doll.

She longs for the noise of the Grands Boulevards,
sees the night-light as a shining Oscar awarded
for the great image of France continually
showing in the cinémathèque of her imagination.

Coveting light, flying ants break their wings
upon the street lamps, fall sinfully to earth
wriggling in worm-like shame, humbled.

As the palm trees sweep the moon away
the houseboy brings morning in the pannier
of his bike. She wakes quickly, full of plans.

THE CIRCUMCISION OF KARL

The world has enough sharpness and danger
yet on every desk we keep the abhorred shears
mocking the outline of the sex they threaten,
one scrotal sac correctly lower than its neighbour.

Intolerable this face they show, calmly bespectacled.
Provoked, we use them dreadfully
poking their eyes out, prising the fine jaws
open to a dolphin's scream.

In Moscow, the street artists
snip out the silhouette of Marx
black and empty,
the Victorian conception of Africa.

Snip, snip, around the crown
and Suez opens to imperial trade.
He approved, making workers of peasants
but knew nothing of the girls, spreadeagled

as the very scissors, opened for the Pharaonic cut.
Try it and see, walk those silvery legs
slowly through the pubic bush
and contemplate the menace of the ordinary.

EXTRACTS FROM THE EVERYDAY HUYSMANS

But when at last his wishes were granted, he suffered immediate and
immeasurable disappointment.

We met in a garden that hovered between
the precious and the earthy: scimitars
of grass polished by silken butterflies
were crudely parted by hens, fussing
with that loping stretch-necked scuttle
of bystanders approaching an accident.

Now sex has us all-at-sea, held under
by our failed dirigible we cling
as we drown, protesting the linen waves
with throat cries. I dread the descent,
the *mal de mer*, these dockside smells,
and lie, dreaming of dry-land,

trying to re-enter the purifying smoke
of burning leaves that hid in the air,
a sudden spice in a bland dish, that day
of sun so white your skin seemed stained,
lemon in an emptied cup, xeroxed
to a mere copy of touchable flesh.

* * *

These gaudy ties are a poisoned aquarium, dead
under glass like something unwholesome in aspic.
The tailor lands one with a fisherman's flick

flat on his counter with that arrogant spread
the butcher uses unfolding liver, his oblation
drawn from some shared catalogue of presentation

the way you impatiently flounce your hair or turn
a page—the theatre of blood. A play
whose message is clear: it's time for me to pay.

I merely paper over the salesman's concern
with these curiously engraved billets-doux
but pour out a harder currency for you.

* * *

Your spices are fragrant, the ashes of a whore
or ingredients for the decadent apothecary.
Without you here I concoct a simpler fare—

the frying pan's a glowing hand mirror
from which two eggs stare back accusingly
at me the interloper. The hot tap has a cold

while ice-cubes boil over in the fridge, now
everything rises in revolt: the kettle whistles
the bacon spits, your toaster rejects my bread.

CHAIRPERSONS

The carnival freaks do it their way:
to the legless man the chairback is a rung
on the ladder he needs to circle the globe,

the Fat Lady covers its insult with a sigh
while for Tom Thumb's Bride it's Carnegie Hall
when, after a deep bow, the Barker steps off.

He alone ignores what they take to be a throne
or a machine, a comment even. Foolishly
he thinks a chair is only a tree sitting down.

DRIVING INFIDELITY

He kissed her breast till blood
strawberried the skin, that sudden fireburst
of a cigarette tossed from a speeding car . . .

the trees hated the headlights, she hated
the red puddles of furry things dying blind,
only relaxing when the dawn's blue steel wove

into a bridge's purl and plain. Now she lies
wary of his mouth's search for the sensations
he believes hide in the corners of her body.

You blew smoke through your nose, thoroughbred
in a frosty field, eyes closed when hedgerows
smeared the windscreen at the bends.

You are afraid of the accidental me
as if I were the shuddering pistons, tearing
hair and skin on the tarmac; shards of glass.

The children know. You take them for a drive
and I watch you go, a man and his family
in a moving gallery of oddly-shaped portraits

yet when their father comes home
they say nothing. At a garage, a rubber tube
draws off our air leaving us in a vacuum of love.

REINCARNATION BY THE SEA

in memory of my grandmother Rachel Sweetman

1 THE OLD CONDITIONS

The veil is windpasted about you, a salt figure
looking back on past happiness, and I remember
your telling me how, after that wedding picture,

grandfather loved only The People, he'd bawl
the Internationale but later come, mindless
to your bed, pendant with ale. Child-death

and the Germans left four of seven he fathered
and you fought to keep them from the 'works.
Now victorious they come to take you, cossetted

as a bride, on outings in their company cars
while he rocks in place, obedient as the lever
in a watch, overlooked by all but time.

2 INHERITANCE

By a beach buckled in the heat,
grandmother rented a chalet
and we were summoned.

My cousins crept off to play snooker
with the intensity of scientists
recreating molecules, scattering genes.

But I stayed, listening to her stories
of the Carl Rosa chorus
while on her hand-cranked gramophone

78s as wide as my arm
turned like the Big Wheel
and, scraped out of their deep lacquer,

Galli-Curci's high coloratura came
with the shriek of any shop girl
going over the top. So we sat

till crabs repossessed the foreshore
puncturing it with dry-rot.
Yet sometimes nightfall saddened her

making her think of lights dimming
in Houses she'd never play again,
seeing the circle's death's-head grin,

a row of boxes, each an eye
closing in the gloom, and then
a spotlight's nimbus for the beckoning angel.

But I was full of sounds
projected into the twilight:
the domes on the pier

were the Pasha's Palace, and Mozart
hid her sense of loss from me.
Today I know I owe her music,

but then, how my beery cousins laughed
at two such humming birds
in their blunt rookery.

3 WINTERING WITH GRANDMOTHER'S MEMORY

Once we saw a man walk mindless
through a glass partition, lightning struck
and he looked down, bemused by angular snow,
bleeding from the force of alchemy, air becoming ice.

c

How clear grandmother's skin became, I thought
I saw life suspended just below its surface
like the bird in flight held in every frozen pool.
Perhaps now her grave is a glacier, imperceptible

her return, mocking the shattering of lives,
already I read messages into a skater's shorthand
but when I think I see her through these cold windows
I go in to the fire and cloud my eyes with hot drinks.

LOVE IN ASIA

In double rows, bombs from a B52 opened
like a zip, an obscenity for your birth
that the women shut out, eyes lowered
to Buddha whose golden hands direct only
celestial traffic. We too postpone truth,

blind to the child pregnant with hunger,
yet fail when silver spoons become
base metal in spiced heat and your hair
slips from my hands, the dark brilliance
only a night sky drowning in ricefields.

ANTONIA BAKUNIN IN SIBERIA

The break-up of Michael's relationships with women usually came about because their physical desire for him broke through the game of spiritual love they were playing and Michael, sensing danger, hastily retreated. *Bakunin*,
ANTHONY MASTERS

Antonia Kwiatkowski loved him when he said
he loved her hands, each the heart-shaped linden leaf,
though he rarely touched them.

Antonia Bakunin saw his, splayed, spiky and foreign,
as he waved goodbye, seeing revolution as a hothouse,
seeding only history with his rampant fist.

Left behind, Antonia pitied the old ladies
wrapping a beggar's hand round a warm cup
pleading for a future in the leaves.

Just once she asked but, mocking
her disbelief, the proffered palm kept silent
though the little lips at every joint

should have whispered something. Even so, she knew
he would never return. Her waiting hands
tried to soothe that hurt, smoothing it

with the sanding sound of skin on skin, until slowly
the deepening lines hardened like the sleigh-tracks
between her and his creative passion.

EMIGRANTS

1 A death in the Old Country . . .

A week after the funeral, kids smashed the windows
that now must hang like school maps of great islands,
while sheet-draped chairs wait
silent as the Roman Senate, its legions gone.
The striped torsos no longer swell with pride
when their drawer is opened
and only that last aerogramme changes,
trying to be an Origami flower on a sandy shelf.

2 . . . but it all seems so far away.

Here, water flogs a lawn green-raw but these boys
are tough and scream with pleasure under the lash.
The veranda TV shows *Coronation Street*, tunnel-vision
to the damp world that sent the telegram,
a pale patch of northern sun hidden from the children.
To them, grandad was merely fog, a grey fiction
when true death is the bird they found once,
with curling legs and perished-rubber eyes.

THAT OLD LEVANTINE BORDELLO

Marie adjusts a black fishnet seam,
the jagged graph of a falling heartbeat,
and flounces the mille-feuilles
of her creamy pantaloons,
she spikes her lashes out sharply
into the rays of dark suns, and leaves
the fossil of a teardrop poised at each ear.

The banquette is velvet plush, dimpled
with a dozen rosy navels, while above,
the elaborate brass fitment
apes a musician's nightmare, a mix
of French horn, tuba and trombone
whose mantles merely hiss
like Eve's python and Cleopatra's asp.

This is the oleograph of wickedness
we cherish, the sepia sins
of the wild fathers we wished we'd had,
pensively weighing a brassière,
a soft Fabergé egg opening to nothing,
or pulling off a glove as if
yanking out the offending fingers.

So we recreate that which we never knew
from Lautrec, Degas, de Maupassant,
fleshing it out with a closer reality—
Louise, the Madame in black bombasine,
surveys her pigeons from a municipal bench
and the monsieur, without the W up his nose,
lives above the corner shop.

AT THE HEART OF A BIG CITY

The last rubber man has bounced away
about to burst with health. A child howls,
its abandoned yacht the shark the ducks acknowledge
with the politeness of Japanese generals.
By the gate, sacks of rubbish with gathered ruffs
squat like so many sad pagliacci,
their pierrot smocks sagging
under the weight of expended happiness.

Back to Antrim Road and a painless concert
from our kitten, the mad harpist,
plucking tunelessly at strings
frayed from the sofa—not exactly Telemann
but enough to distract us from the noise upstairs:
a girl beaten by her lover. She never protests
but tomorrow, dead leaves will lie
beneath the frost of make-up she must wear.

THE SHORT HISTORY OF FAILED IDEAS

Franz Anton Mesmer 1734–1815

Sheep advance across their heft,
drawn by the rusty horse-shoe
pinned to the gate. Rich and poor
experience this animal magnetism,
those with stained wool hanging
in the filthy ringlets of slum children
and those in their elegant cardigans.

One despairs of cure, bloated on clover
it lies in its Tolstoy shirt
waiting for the true physician,
the shepherd with a sharpened stave.
The others go on, feeling the pull
this way and that, this way and that
drawn by the old rusty horse-shoe.

Alfred Wegener 1880–1930

With comic menace
the fruit on the sampans
is laid out military style:

the papaya's caveman club
or the durian's antique
mustard-gas grenade.

The tourists enjoy the joke
until one is offered a coconut
lopped like a temple novice

with milk that looks so maternal
they turn away disgusted.
They prefer a more abstract beverage

and only the coke tins
with tear-drop openings
seem sad at their leaving—

for this is the new Gondwanaland,
the adhesive white world rejoining
the continents, the Yin and Yang,

snug as chops in a pan,
and the airport runways
are ley lines that link us all.

WILHELM REICH 1897–1957

The man in the raincoat enters
the red orgone box, presses
the instrument to his head . . .

drring, drring—drring, drring—
and at once, the primal
mass-free energy strikes.

Renewed, he yearns to try,
any number will do . . .
drring, drring—drring, drring—

but the cure has taxed his strength
and all that comes is his heavy breathing . . .
hurr, hurr—hurr, hurr—

CARL JUNG 1875–1961

Her first premonition, a feather on an egg,
was the last of Icarus on Dædalus' skull. Next,
a spray of bird droppings under the eaves

she saw as the molten wax, the day
was hot enough. In the end it happened
while walking home from church: an old cow

alone, unbidden, trundled up between
the narrow hedgerows—the minotaur in drag
defeated by the green labyrinth; lost in age.

Suddenly she hates this well-read deceit,
she has seen the six-legged dog and why
it danced was clear, but terrifying, she runs

to the playground and swings high, clutching
the chains, Pasiphaë in the unrelenting machine,
the rapid to and fro safely sheathed in myth.

JOURNEY TO THE END OF THE LAND

A wigwam each. A burned-out covered wagon
with burned-out toast. The two saloon girls
in silver crinolines survived the blaze
but it's still too hot to bury the dead,

the coffins melt and smell like Brie.
You spread the map, looking West,
while I go to check the quotidian miracle:
water in the radiator turned to wine.

All journeys end or begin in this
last carpark, our final chance to rent
a piece of England. We photograph each other
thinking about America, turn and go back again.

IO TRIUMPHE

If the wall itches
the spiders scratch it
for this is our symbiotic world:

the make-up cat dusts her powder puff
across the Mercedes' warm cheek
and only the humans are out of sorts.
Look at her

trying to adjust the vertical hold
on his suit while he grapples
with the old school python.

For a moment last night
they scratched and dusted
the warm itch,
now his first cigarette

stubs into her combed-out hairs
which flash in the ash-tray
like the warning flax—

Homine te momente . . .
Now look at the radio
so full of itself it bursts
out laughing.

Lizard-pouchy, wading off Dartmoor
his rifle balanced to assay its worth
and when he pushes his beret up
blackened features end like a lopped egg.

A fisted cigarette gutters, first fire
in a shallow cave, first defence
for the streets of bright houses
each a face, unaware of fear, being ninety

or nothing in an instant. Light now,
where Friesians wait milk-heavy,
their continents a reminder of half a world
waking, a suicide club. The sun picks out

the anorexic puppets dangling to the horizon,
simpletons who carry the screams of the powerful
in a language of chattering teeth. Grumbling,
a jeep comes, its aerials fishing hope

from the sharp air; yes, this violence
is everywhere possible but today elsewhere,
not here in this treasury of gold-
dusted gorse far from the target cities.

TWO YOUNG MEN, A DECEMBER TRAIN

One, holding his book like a rice bowl
so his eyes can pick out words, steady
while the other impersonates age and infirmity.

Like cocoons stirring, the date stones
dance on the ledge by his hand: strange
how each finger reflects the crescent moon.

One sways, a prince in a howdah; one watches.
They look out to see themselves, sprinkled
with cheap glitter, Magi on a Christmas card.

Suspecting they are gay, a lady in the corridor
begins to twitch her coat, pointedly,
as if it were a curtain in the suburbs.

Noisy as a factory, a passing train
projects its out-of-frame film show. Laughing,
they watch other silent lovers acting them.

COLD BEDS

Thirty years she had waited for disaster
and when they told her he had drowned
she nodded. Like things seen in Holy prints

there had been signs: the greengrocer
piling bound asparagus as if to burn a saint
made her cross herself quickly.

And when she took flowers for Bob
a dead gull lay on the boy's grave,
plump and grey as the shell that killed him.

So now the father's gone, after thirty years
on a bed too big for one she sees it all:
the sails becalmed at the window,

her Madonna for a prow, the moonlight
that gives their walnut cupboard the pattern
of waves closing over his head.